D1755273

South Beach
Tales and Poems

Terry Tracht

SOUTH BEACH TALES AND POEMS

Terry Tracht

Photography by Irene Sperber

ISBN (Print Edition): 978-1-66784-899-0

ISBN (eBook Edition): 978-1-66784-900-3

© 2022. All rights reserved. No part of this publication may be reproduced, distributed, or transmitted in any form or by any means, including photocopying, recording, or other electronic or mechanical methods, without the prior written permission of the publisher, except in the case of brief quotations embodied in critical reviews and certain other noncommercial uses permitted by copyright law.

For

Roman, Jason and Amanda,

who continually inspire me.

ABOUT THE AUTHOR

TERRY TRACHT was born in Brooklyn, NY, raised on a farm in Vineland, NJ, and spent her teens in her parents' pinball arcade on the Atlantic City Boardwalk. Terry holds a Bachelor of Arts degree in Psychology and Sociology from Douglass College, Rutgers University, a Master of Science in Management degree from Florida International University and a Juris Doctorate degree from the University of Miami School of Law. She enjoys writing short stories and poetry, and as her favorite subjects are her family members, her work is often laced with humor. Terry loves to travel and has accompanied her husband Roman on several cross country motorcycle trips. She resides in Miami Beach with him and their beloved beagle Brandy.

This is her third book. Some stories have been remastered.

South Beach
Tales and Poems

Contents

PARADISE 1

SOUTH BEACH LIVING 2

FOR AMANDA 3

MARK MY WORDS 5

MY SON 8

MOVING ON 9

THE RUNNER 11

SUNRISE 12

A DAY AT THE "J" 14

MZ 16

ON SECOND THOUGHT 17

IRMA WAS NO LADY 18

BEACH HARDWARE 25

THE BIRTHDAY PARTY 27

PARADISE

Sunshine bathes this expansive beach,

highlighting a long row of geometric hotels which have stood the test of time.

It is a place where tourists become the primary residents.

They have packed their worries into stuffed suitcases,

hoping that the sun will melt their cares away.

Their roasting bodies turn as if on rotisseries atop Walgreens beach towels.

They are quite a sight,

recovering from a whiskey-fueled night.

They lie there as the sea makes love to the shore,

ebbing, retracting and then spilling its salty foam onto the sand.

The aroma of Cuban coffee permeates the air.

Bicyclists speed by to no one knows where.

The taste of mango sweetens the day.

Here and there are abandoned ones along the way.

Drivers are not intimidated by fancy cars blasting their horns.

They take their time.

They know that eventually we all wind up at the same red light.

Hurricanes with Spanish names may threaten this paradise,

but living here is worth the price.

Young, leggy Russian girls slink across trendy nightclub floors.

Their provocative eyes beckon older men, hoping to have not only a good time, but also a good life.

One's wildest dreams seem to be within reach, in the unreality that is South Beach.

SOUTH BEACH LIVING

Oh, the things you can do in South Beach,

the many ways you can play.

You can frolic on the island the entire day.

Order a steamy cafe' con leche

and a tostada Cubana,

nurse a frozen pina colada,

finally learn how to salsa.

On Lincoln Road

you can purchase food galore,

satisfying the taste buds

of gourmet connoisseurs.

To savor the flavor

of locals' favorite haunt,

indulge in dinner at

Joe's Stone Crab Restaurant.

A variety of activities are available for free,

such as Ocean Drive concerts

and wallcasts of the New World Symphony.

Last but not least,

and perhaps the most fun,

is relaxing on white, sandy beaches

under the South Beach sun.

FOR AMANDA

I don't want to admit it,

but it is true.

I spend hours a day thinking of you.

I envision the long waves of your honey blonde hair,

and your slightly freckled face so fair.

I see you standing tall and lean

with gold flecked eyes of bright blue-green.

Before your visit

it had been quite a while

since I had seen

your dimpled smile.

So delightful it was

having you near,

because we only get to see each other

about twice a year.

We spent three days together

doing what we do best-

enjoying South Beach's sun-soaked weather

and conducting restaurant taste tests.

We played lengthy games of scrabble

and 500 rummy,

and you beat me so badly,

that I felt like a dummy.

Soon it was time for you to leave

and I didn't want to say good-bye,

but I kept my emotions in check

and my heart held high.

I gave you a long, tight hug at the airport

and you went on your way

back home to Colorado,

where you plan to indefinitely stay.

MARK MY WORDS

Sam and I first saw each other at a meeting of South Beach Toastmasters Club. The mission of the Toastmasters was to build self-confidence, communication skills and leadership through impromptu public speaking. It met each week for about an hour, during which we would be asked to speak for one to two minutes on a subject for which we had no advance preparation. Sam and I felt that these skills would be an asset to our private as well as professional lives.

During our first time attending, Sam was asked to give a short speech about global warming. He knew little about it, but he was composed and self-confident when he addressed the group for his two minutes of fame. It did not escape me that he was also good looking: tall, trim, warm amber eyes and a cute, slightly crooked smile. I found him quite charming. The attraction seemed to be mutual, as following the meeting, Sam asked me to go for a drink with him at the nearby Algonquin Hotel. I accepted his invitation. The Hotel had an elegant but cozy lounge where many a deal was consummated by area businessmen and attorneys. Time flew over drinks as we discussed everything from politics to art. Sam was a consultant with the firm of Byrnes and Young and he was single, having tragically lost his wife in a car crash ten months prior. He had no children. He admitted that he had not been with a woman since the death of his wife and couldn't even imagine being in a relationship, as his loss was still painfully fresh. He would go to work, come home, eat a take-out dinner and go to bed and begin the next day anew. I had compassion for his loneliness.

I had not dated in months following a bad breakup with a long-time boyfriend. I didn't have much luck with online dating and had pretty much resigned myself to being single and just concentrate on my work as a guardian ad litem for the State of Florida. Sam was the first man to spark my interest. We continued to meet for drinks at the Algonquin after our weekly

Toastmasters meetings. Drinks eventually turned into dinners and our friendship grew into something more.

About two months after we met, Sam and I went to Le Rivage Restaurant in Coral Gables, where we enjoyed a delicious filet mignon dinner and a few too many glasses of fine French wine. Afterward, he suggested that we get a room in the Algonquin and I agreed.

Sam turned out to be a skilled but gentle lover and he knew just how to please me. He was filled with longing and his desire was insatiable. I could tell that he was a man who had not been with a woman in a while. We made passionate love throughout the night and he caused my body to ache with pleasure. Eventually, I fell asleep in his arms, but my fulfillment was short-lived, as Sam gently woke me because he had to prepare for an important presentation at work the next morning. I had to be in court for an 8a.m. hearing, so it was for the best.

We left the hotel and Sam walked me to my car parked in front of the Toastmasters Club headquarters. He wrapped his arms around my waist and drew me in like a magnet. He held me tightly, looked into my eyes and admitted, "I think I am falling in love with you." His lips crashed into mine and he kissed me deeply and intensely. My heart was pounding wildly and my knees nearly gave out from under me.

And then I saw it: a Lexus SUV parked across the street, its engine running. A dark-haired woman sat inside. Suddenly, she swung the door open and jumped out of the vehicle in such haste, that she left the engine on and the door ajar. She was on fire and ran across the street screaming at Sam:

"You bastard! This is why you've been coming home late? This is how you treat your wife after twelve years of marriage?"

"This is what you do to our three daughters? And you, you bitch," she snarled at me, "You're nothing but a husband-stealing whore!"

Shivers ran down my spine and a wave of nausea engulfed me. I frantically searched Sam's face for answers, but he did not look at me. Instead, he stood there sheepishly with his head down, staring at his feet.

I blurted out, "He lied to both of us! I had no idea that he was married, let alone the father of three children."

The woman's eyes were crazed with fury. "Stay away from my husband and get out of my sight, you bitch," she hissed at me. She then gave me a forceful shove. I nearly toppled to the sidewalk, but caught myself. I was shaken, but I forgave her anger. I wanted to apologize for the pain I inadvertently had caused her. But when I looked at her tortured face, I turned around and walked away instead.

MY SON

You were so sweet when you were small.

You hardly troubled me at all.

With twinkling eyes of chocolate brown,

you were such a joy to have around.

I'd push your stroller through Pine Tree Park

and stop at the fountain to look for sharks.

You grew from precocious child to young boy to man,

always ready to lend me a hand.

I was so proud of you when you began to teach

in an A+ school right on South Beach.

Twelve years living at home you spent,

saving money on exorbitant rent.

Then one day you moved away

to a bachelor pad where we thought you'd stay.

It had a great location, a huge gym and deep pool,

which all of the ladies thought was cool.

But not long after, you changed your mind,

leaving all of those costly amenities behind.

Now my living room is stuffed with

your boxes, sofa, table and chairs,

a tv, computer and kitchen wares.

I'd never guess that at 33,

you'd move back home to live with me.

MOVING ON

It finally happened and you did it all alone.
The time had come for you to leave home.
It was years in the making and very painstaking,
but now there was no doubt.
You were going to move out.

You searched high and low for a place you'd like to go.
Not just anywhere would do.
North Miami, Miami Shores and Wynwood were too
far from the action for you.

You finally found a condo on South Beach,
where all of the clubs and young people were within your reach.
Your father and I met the news with glee.
We delighted in the thought that we'd finally be free.

After one year of living there alone,
you fell in love and moved into your girlfriend's home.
It wasn't hard for anyone to see that you and she were meant to be.
You, the little boy that I used to carry,
were all grown up and going to get married.

You exchanged vows with your beautiful wife
and then moved on to start a new life.
It hasn't been that long since you've been gone,
yet I feel so alone with just your dad and I at home.

I miss you asking me about my day.

I miss seeing your car in the driveway.

I'll miss you taking the puppy for her morning walks.

I'll miss going to movie premieres with you and our late-night talks.

There are no more shoes by the door,

no full laundry baskets on the floor.

I sit next to your empty chair.

I envision your smile, and you aren't there.

THE RUNNER

His hair is thick and brown with gold tipped curls. A caramel colored tan covers his chiseled body. He runs, hazel eyes focused, not along the flat shoreline, but on the lumpy gray sand, which is no match for his Adonis-like legs. Around his neck rests a thick link chain from which hangs a large golden medallion. It claps against his broad, hairless chest as he runs, revealing a cross etched into one side and a six pointed star on the other. He jogs early each morning at about the same time. A handful of beach-going groupies regularly gather on Miami Beach's 14th Street beach to admire him. The runner's strides are long and stag like, exhibiting strength, determination and grace. He runs until he is a dot in the distance. After what seems like a long absence to his spectators, he winds down, finally returning to his starting point. He breathes deeply, his muscular chest heaving, as he circles the blue and white striped towel he had left behind on the sand. Shaking it off, he places it around his wide neck. He slides his feet into open toed, calf leather sandals and walks to the boardwalk with an air of confidence, as his devotees follow him with their eyes. He skips up 10 steep, wooden steps to the boardwalk, turns left and continues walking south until he disappears from view. He is gone-at least until tomorrow. A stranger has once more made my day and he doesn't even know it.

SUNRISE

My husband Roman was born and raised in Tashkent, the capitol of Uzbekistan, a Central Asian nation and former Soviet republic. Uzbekistan borders on Turkmenistan, Tajikistan and Afganistan, and is one of only two countries in the world which is doubly landlocked. Eighty percent of the country's territory is comprised of monotonous desert, and the only visible bodies of water there are occasional lakes and man-made reservoirs. Roman only knew what the Atlantic and Pacific Oceans and Caribbean Sea looked like from maps. He could never imagine experiencing the sea firsthand.

My husband considered cruise ships to be "floating prisons with excess food," and it took me months of coaxing to convince him to book us on a seven-day voyage to the Caribbean. We sailed aboard Royal Caribbean's *Oasis of the Seas,* which accommodates 5,600 travelers and is one of the largest passenger ships in the world. Roman was left wide-eyed by the vessel's five saltwater pools, gigantic twisting water slide, three whirlpools and its "Central Park" themed boardwalk, but being a Uzbek stoic, he did not express his approval. We had a balcony cabin on the seventh deck. It was tighter than we expected, but comfortable enough for two, and it was appointed with amenities such as down pillows, plush terry cloth bathrobes, soft slippers and Penhaligon soaps from London.

During our first dinner aboard, we savored a scrumptious buffet of culinary delights ranging from shrimp tacos to Peking duck to delicious, rare roast beef. This was accompanied by a vast selection of fresh salads, tropical fruits, free flowing, soft ice cream and mouth watering desserts such as seven layer caramel cake and white chocolate mousse. Roman didn't admit it, but by his several trips to the dessert station, I knew he was impressed. After dinner, we headed to the Opal Theater, where we enjoyed a lavish stage production of the Broadway musical "CATS," which we viewed from our plush, red velvet seats. To top the evening off, we relaxed over frozen pina coladas in the 24 hour cocktail lounge adjacent to the Casino. By 1:30 a.m., we were bushed and called it a night.

On our first morning at sea, I awakened to a sliver of bright light seeping between our slightly drawn curtains. I pulled open the long silk drapes and was captivated by an intoxicating sight I had never experienced from such a vantage point. My eyes scanned an expansive, powder-blue sky dotted with puffs of billowing cotton. After a few moments, I watched in awe as a golden glow crept over the horizon. Then, ever so slowly, it emerged- a fiery coral orb. Its rays radiated from its core, illuminating the sea below.

I had to adjust to the brightness of the orange sphere from the comparative darkness of our cabin. My eyes ached as I stared at it, but I could not look away. I was mesmerized by the vision and felt it would be selfish of me not to share the moment with my husband. I approached my sleeping partner, leaned in and called his name. I had learned a long time ago, the hard way, not to touch him while he slept.

"Honey, wake up and come to the balcony. You have got to see this sunrise," I said. He was lying face down on his stomach, his long darkbrown hair teasing his bare, broad shoulders. He didn't respond. After a few moments, I gingerly called his name again. He did not move, but with a voice muffled by his pillow, he muttered:

"I don't know why you bother me with these things. They have better ones in Tashkent."

A Day at the "J"

Since my trip to visit my daughter in Denver, I had been waking up between 2 to 3a.m. due to the time change. I'd brew myself a strong cup of coffee and just stay up ordering t-shirts online from GAP that I didn't need and shop from the Macy's catalog for over-priced jewelry that I'd subsequently return. If I was really motivated, I'd bake my husband's favorite cherry-raisin banana bread, even though he wasn't around to eat it.

Finally, I thought I had gotten a good night of sleep after taking a nap and waking up at 6:45, just in time to get ready for my 7:30 a.m. water aerobics class. I had the convenience of living adjacent to the Miami Beach JCC, where I attended the class four days a week.

I quickly donned my swimsuit, swim pants and rash guard, packed a towel, applied sunblock to my face and put on my hat and sunglasses. I poured breakfast into my beagle Brandy's bowl and rushed out of the door.

It was a lovely morning, warm but not too humid, with cloudless, azure skies. As I approached the JCC, I was surprised to see that its gate was padlocked with a thick metal chain. I stood there for a few moments, not quite knowing what to do. I thought there might have been some emergency, but I saw no police cars. I didn't have my phone with me and couldn't make a call, so I just returned home.

When I walked through the front door, Brandy, who had been perched on top of the sofa staring at me from out of our picture window, gave me a quizzical look. Wearing my hat and sunglasses, with my bag still slung over my shoulder, I quickly phoned the JCC's front desk. No one answered. I opened the door to have another look and I noticed that the skies had darkened. Then I realized what was happening. The clock on my living room wall indicated 7:15, but instead of it being Sunday morning, it was still Saturday evening! No wonder passersby had given me strange looks as I hurried past them in my hat and dark sunglasses.

Brandy leaped onto my bed waiting for me to follow. We had been enjoying going to sleep early, since my husband was in Moscow and not there to criticize me for doing so. I wiped the sunblock from my face and entertained the idea of jumping into bed fully clothed, ready to go to water aerobics in the morning, just in case I overslept. But I decided against it, changed into my pj's and joined Brandy, who was curled up in a nest she fashioned from my pillows, and was looking at me contentedly, probably wondering what she did to deserve an extra meal on Saturday night.

When I told my son and daughter what had occurred, they greeted my story with laughter and disbelief. "Don't you have a single clock in the house which indicates AM or PM?" my son wanted to know. "Why couldn't you have asked Alexa?" my daughter chimed in. I suppose either would have been a good idea, but I had no doubt as to the accuracy of my orientation. I felt fully refreshed from what I thought was a good night of sleep and was encouraged to get ready for water aerobics by the light and welcoming skies that I had seen from my windows.

The kids must have relayed all of this to my husband, who, the following evening, phoned me from Russia to inform me that the current time in the U.S. was 6:30 pm and not 6:30 am. Feeling my face flush at my family's chiding, I vowed not to make the same mistake in the future. So, several days days later when I happened to awaken at twilight, I took no chances. I approached Alexa and asked her: "Alexa, what time is it in Miami Beach?" She cheerfully replied, "It is 7:30 p.m. Enjoy the sunrise, Terry." I couldn't believe my ears. *Was she actually teasing me?*

Bewildered, I phoned my son. "Jason," I gasped, "I know you are not going to believe me, but Alexa just informed me that it was 7:30 p.m. and told me to enjoy the sunrise. Am I losing my mind?" He let out a hearty laugh. "Mom, you obviously did not hear her correctly. Alexa told you to enjoy the SUNSET, not the sunrise."

"Oh, then never mind," I replied apologetically, and then I jumped into bed.

MZ

I thought this is the way it would always be:

sharing, caring, you and me.

The weekends were always loaded with fun:

a marathon of movies, laughter, soaking up the poolside sun.

But then one day a crate came from overseas,

parts of the motorcycle you ordered, a German MZ.

For days, you painstakingly assembled it.

Screw by screw. Bit by bit.

You hardly had time to speak to me.

And that was the beginning of what was to be.

On the day you twisted in the last bolt, you beamed with pride.

You said, "See you in a few hours, honey. I'm taking her for a ride."

The bikers at South Beach Cycle Shop became your new friends.

And you went riding with them

almost every weekend.

And so, I felt very much alone.

As you, my new husband, were hardly ever home.

I was once so fulfilled with us as two.

But now we are three:

you, me and that damned MZ.

ON SECOND THOUGHT

It came with a cushy passenger seat,

and special pegs on which to put my feet.

It was cherry red, shiny and new,

and you wanted me to ride with you.

You bought me a silver motorcycle suit,

which made me look fat,

but you said it looked cute.

You got me a silver helmet, too,

so I'd match, sitting in back of you.

I just don't like to breathe in the helmet's stale air.

I don't like the way that it mats down my hair.

I would never ride on I95.

We'd be lucky to get off it alive.

You tried to convince me with all of your might,

and you could not get me to hop on that bike.

In your black leather gear you looked so sleek,

getting ready for Daytona Bike Week.

But when I think about it,

watching bike races may not be so bad.

It could be the best time I ever had.

Unless I try it, I'll never know.

So ask me to come, and I will go!

IRMA WAS NO LADY

It was Wednesday, September 6, 2017, and I was glued to CNN, fearfully monitoring Hurricane Irma, the most intense and widespread hurricane since Hurricane Dean in 2007. The entire state of Florida was engulfed by its projected cone. With horror, I soon learned that Miami was to be a direct hit of this Category 5 event. Not surprisingly, Miami Beach residents received an order to evacuate. My son Jason, an elementary school teacher, left his South Beach apartment to be with me as my husband Roman was in Georgia, camping with friends.

Our house was not hurricane ready. We had meant to buy shutters, but never got around to it. The wood boards which we had previously purchased had rotted and we disposed of them. Our living room had four large windows which had been installed years before, and were not hurricane resistant. It was too late to find anyone to buy plywood and to board them up. They could shatter, and subsequent wind pressure could create a vacuum and lift up our roof. At the least, the roof would incur substantial damage, for our lackadaisical roofer had removed more than a dozen clay tiles days ago and abandoned them. He had never returned to patch a leak we had over our bedroom. He was scheduled to complete the work on Monday, September 4th, but typical of Miami contractors, he never showed up nor did he return any of my calls. The tiles could become projectiles in the wind and cause damage to our property or that of our neighbor, who was not shy to insinuate that he'd have no problem suing us if they did. They had to be removed. Dear Jason, who did not like heights, had to climb a ladder two stories to the roof to pick up the custom made tiles, and toss them to me one at a time. I would then place them into the shed.

Worse perhaps than the wind, was that six to eleven feet of water surge was predicted. Our living room would be inundated with flood waters, swallowing everything in their path. We had little time. *What to save?* I asked myself.

I glanced at my large wedding portrait which adorned the living room wall. It was much too large and cumbersome to bring with us. But I'd never look that good again, so I had Jason carry it to safety up our winding stairs to the second floor. *What else?*

I had hundreds of pictures of Jason and my daughter Amanda which filled more than 15 albums of memories. I placed them into white, 13 gallon garbage bags, and shoved them into my closets on top of my clothes. They would be safe from a four foot water surge, I reasoned. Ultimately, I decided to take my wedding album and the kids' bar and bat mitzvah tapes with us.

So where to go? Naples? Atlanta? Tampa? It was difficult to predict where it would be safest to avoid the wrath of Irma, who was a very fickle lady.

Jason reasoned that Orlando would be best as it was inland. And it just so happened that his newly married best friend had recently relocated from Miami Beach to a new highrise building in the center of downtown. Mike and Janet wholeheartedly invited us to ride out the storm with them. Their modern two bedroom / two bath condo was located between Colonial Drive and Orange Ave. and they were its first occupants. Jason would sleep on his camping cot in the small second bedroom, which had been converted into an office. I would spend nights on a queen size blow-up mattress on the floor of the living room, which had floor to ceiling windows. I voiced concern about being surrounded by sheets of glass, but Jason assured me that, according to Mike, the windows were hurricane impact resistant.

We settled in, using pillows, sheets and towels we had brought with us. I had packed five cans of tuna, two jars each of peanut butter and jelly, a loaf of whole wheat bread and five gallons of purified water.

Mike was a bit obsessive compulsive and kept rearranging the order of the food I placed on top of his kitchen counter. He also added cream and sugar to our coffee according to his taste, and Jason and I could barely drink it. One day we even had a disagreement about butter.

I had saved a few pats from lunch at a diner and put them into the fridge. When I needed to use butter later, Mike took out his margarine, telling me that it was the best and insisted that I use it instead. Fortunately, Jason came to my rescue, convincing him that I get severe indigestion from margarine.

We had our own bathroom, which was great. But I was somewhat unnerved when I found our used towels neatly folded on the towel rack, when we had hung them over the shower rod to dry.

After a couple of days of reprieve, Irma smacked Orlando as a Category 1 storm, packing winds of about 74 mph. *Piece of* cake, I thought, compared to the monster tempest which was predicted to lash Miami. From the living room's picture windows, we saw the wind whip the branches of the trees, many of which fractured. I watched as the torrential rain filled the parking lot across the street with large pools of water. We expected to be plunged into darkness at any moment, but fortunately we never lost power. We were all happy to spend the idle hours just watching CNN and snacking.

The next morning, at about 4:45am, I was awakened by the sound of someone fumbling at the front door. The knob rattled loudly, accompanied by incessant clicking of the lock. Whoever was out there tried to force his key into the cylinder repeatedly. I begged to myself, *Please don't let him open the door.* It wouldn't be hard to do, as Mike and Janet did not invest in a door chainguard. Apparently, they deemed living in Orlando safer than living in Miami. The rattling and clicking seemed to be getting louder. I hesitantly got up and went to look through the peephole, but I could not make out anything in the dark. My heart pounded as I raced to Jason's room. I abruptly opened his door and screamed in a whisper, "Jay, someone is trying to break in!" Jason shot up, his lips trembling slightly. "Jay, wake up Mike," I insisted. Jason sprang from his cot and walked toward the front door. "No, no. Don't go out there," I hoarsely pleaded while digging my nails into his arm. "He may have a gun!" Shrugging my arm away, Jason dauntlessly walked to the door and peered through the peephole. He then quickly unlocked the door, turned the knob and yanked the door open, as I huddled in a corner, holding my breath.

"Mom, there's no one out here. It's just the wind," Jason explained. I timidly stuck my head out into the empty corridor. My son was right. "Now can I go back to bed?" Jason asked tiredly and not without a tinge of sarcasm. My nerves were still frayed. "Jay, can I please sleep here with you?" I begged. "Mom, don't be silly. Go back to bed," he ordered.

In the morning, Jason told Mike and Janet what had happened. "Oh yeh," chuckled Mike, "The door does make weird noises sometimes due to the wind." *Thanks a lot,* I said to myself. *Why didn't you say something about that a little earlier?*

We would spend a total of five days at Mike and Janet's. By that time, I'm sure that they would welcome being able to use their living room, which had been totally engulfed by the queen size mattress they had provided me. And I would welcome the privacy of my own bedroom and not being force fed margarine and coffee creamer by Mike. I had enjoyed our time in Orlando, having sampled the fare of many cozy restaurants in the neighborhood, meals which we treated Mike and Janet to as a form of gratitude for their hospitality.

We left Orlando on Tuesday, September 12th, at 4 a.m., about the same time that we had left Miami to drive there on September 6th. We took I95, after hearing that the Turnpike was backed up at each service plaza by lines of cars which had stopped for gas and were spilling onto the road, blocking the left lane. It was a relatively uneventful ride, until Jason said, "Mom, I have something to tell you but I don't want you to be mad." "What?" I asked. "Well, Mike's windows are not hurricane proof. Mike and I were afraid to tell you earlier; we thought you'd freak out." "I certainly would not have slept next to sweeping sheets of glass, had I known," I said. "How could you do that to your own mother?" I asked, not really joking.

The highway had been cleared, but we could see the ravages of Irma. Huge trees had snapped like twigs and lay defeated on the side of the road. Those palms which were lucky enough to survive, waved limp fronds shredded by Irma's violent winds. It took us five and one-half hours to reach Miami Beach. The vista of the city had drastically changed. In front of each home were piles of tree trunks and foliage. Mounds of debris disfigured front lawns.

Our street, Pine Tree Drive, looked like a battleground. Traffic lights were out, many hanging by their wires. For the drivers we encountered, obeying obligatory four way stop signs was merely optional. When we pulled up to our driveway, I gasped. The bountiful crimson and rose bougainvillea trees, which had adorned the front of our house for over 30 years, were uprooted, brown and scrawny and entirely blocked our metal front gate, which was ajar. Perhaps it was a mixed blessing that we couldn't pass through the thorny barrier. If we couldn't, then no one else could either.

We saw one of our neighbors clip off dead, thick branches and heap them into a mountain on his swale. He kindly agreed to lend Jason his industrial quality clippers and my son went to work, cutting enough branches to allow us to slip through our gate sideways. The wind must have been furious because it had pushed the gate out of its lock and had broken it. The wooden fence which separated our lot from our neighbors was splintered and half of it leaned on top of the adjacent bushes which traversed the property line. Other than that, a broken fuse box door and some missing roof tiles were the extent of our damages. We felt lucky not to have experienced the devastation of our west coast brethren.

Our home had no power and the notion that we would be spending the night in darkness and heat was daunting. Jason actually was invited to stay with a colleague, but I didn't have anywhere to go. I tried to coax an invitation from our neighbor, who happened to have power as evidenced by her bright outdoor lights. Debbie and I attended the same water aerobics classes, exchanged recipes and had shopped many Bloomies clearance sales together. I considered her to be a good friend. Having charged my cell phone in Jason's car, I texted her. Her response was empathetic, so when she invited me over, I thought she was going to offer me one of her two vacant guest rooms for the night. Instead, she walked me into her kitchen, took out a Tupperware container from her cabinet and filled it with ice. "This should help cool you off," she remarked, handing it to me.

We did not want to leave the house unoccupied with its gate open and fence down, so we stayed home that night. Over time, I had collected an arsenal of candles, which I lit and positioned around the living room. Our beds were covered with paintings, vases and figurines we had attempted to elevate before leaving the house. Too exhausted to put things back into their rightful places, we covered the couches with sheets and slept on them-or at least, we tried to. After two hours of tossing, turning and sweating, I took a cold shower by candlelight. But it wasn't long before I was hot again. "Are you ok, Mom?" Jason wanted to know. I was breathing heavily and hoping that I would not pass out from the heat. "I'm fine," I lied, "but this is the last night that I am going to sleep here without air conditioning." We both suffered through the night.

The next morning, I made instant coffee on our gas stove, using the water we had brought back from Orlando. Our neighborhood stores were boarded up and closed, so peanut butter and jelly sandwiches were the breakfast fare.

That afternoon, Jason received a call from a mother whose son was a student in his second grade gifted class. She was considerate enough to inquire how he was weathering the after effects of Irma. When he told her that we had no power, she graciously offered her home to us on Venetian Island. She told Jason that she had a private, waterfront cottage which we could occupy. It sounded great, so we went. Upon arrival, we saw that the front lawn of the house was covered with thick brush and fallen trees, as the family recently returned from a vacation in Italy, and hadn't had time to clear it. The house was a majestic, two story, caramel colored residence hugging Biscayne Bay. Mrs. Lombardi heartily welcomed us. She pointed to a painfully long spiral staircase and said, "Your rooms are upstairs." I was doubly disappointed. First, I couldn't imagine conquering that winding flight of narrow stairs. Secondly, *Where was the cottage?* It turns out that we were given adjacent bedrooms, Jason sharing his with her seven year old son, who had just been released from the hospital following an acute case of bronchitis, and was still coughing severely. Over a spaghetti dinner she prepared, I leaned over to my son and whispered, "We have to get out of here."

As luck would have it, at Debbie's suggestion, I had left the kitchen light switch in the "on" position at home.

With amazing good fortune and exquisite timing, at 7p.m. I received a text from her which read, "Let there be light." Our power was back on!

We excused ourselves from the dinner table and out we flew from the mansion with an abundance of gratitude.

We were going home: back to central air conditioning, back to light and back to our lives. Good riddance, Irma!

BEACH HARDWARE

I suppose I needed more restraint

on the day I decided to shop for paint.

I went to the grand re-opening

of Beach Hardware Store,

which featured products by Benjamin Moore.

It was located on 21st Street,

and advertised prices

that were hard to beat.

Its paints were among the very best,

and were 50% off for cans

$30 or less.

The store even provided a free BBQ spread

catered by a company called

"The Great Big Red."

I walked through the endless isles

searching for painting supplies

and was approached by an attractive man

with a welcoming smile.

As I reached for paint from a top shelf,

he squatted down beside me and asked,

"Hello, pretty lady, can I help?"

"Of course," I excitedly replied,

practically drowning in his hazel green eyes.

He must have been in his mid 40's, that's all.

He had brown wavy hair, broad shoulders

and was tall.

He carried the items I chose to the register for me,

and waited while I browsed patiently.

He kept smiling broadly

and was unusually nice.

He even told the cashier to charge me

the contractor's price.

He then said,

"Pretty lady, these bags are too heavy for you to go very far."

"I insist that you allow me to take them to your car."

After he placed the goods into my trunk,

he turned to face me.

I leaned against my car door provocatively.

"How can I EVER repay you?"

"You're so wonderful," I gushed,

feeling my legs turn into mush.

"It is my pleasure," he said.

"I think that you're a real cutie."

"Besides, I feel that assisting the elderly

is my civic duty."

THE BIRTHDAY PARTY

Attending a birthday dinner during a pandemic is not an easy task.

It's hard to chew and swallow while keeping on a mask.

Eighteen invited guests made up the scene,

and all were required to have had their vaccines.

The hostess tried to assure everyone in the place,

that the waiters were healthy and that they would be safe.

The participants came there to celebrate.

They wanted to scream and to shout,

because it had been over two years

since any of them had been out.